P9-CQP-902

Stuart Robertson

BOOK ORDER FORM

There are two ways that you may order additional copies of "Dear Dr. Humor." You may use the order form provided on the web page at www.drhumor.com or you may photocopy this page, complete the information, enclose a check made out to: National Association for the Humor Impaired Press and mail it to: 3356 Bayside Court, Suite 201, La Crosse, WI 54601. The cost is $12.00 per book which includes postage and handling.

★★

Name: _____

Address: _____

_____

Thank You for Your Order!

Dear Dr. Humor

A Collection of Humorous Stories for All Occasions

compiled
by

Dr. Stuart Robertshaw, CEO
National Association for the Humor Impaired

www.drhumor.com

Published by
The National Association for the Humor Impaired Press
3356 Bayside Court, Suite 201
La Crosse, WI 54601
ISBN 0-9645793-0-8 ©1995

Second Printing, 1996
Third Printing, 1997
Fourth Printing, 1997
Fifth Printing, 1999
Sixth Printing, 2001
Seventh Printing, 2003
Eighth Printing, 2004
Ninth Printing, 2008

ACKNOWLEDGEMENTS

My sincerest appreciation to all those people from around the country who took the time to write and to share their favorite humorous stories. Every time I speak to an audience on the many benefits of humor, I encourage members of the audience to share funny events that have happened to them or to share one of their favorite stories. Those who take the time to write are given a free lifetime membership kit, celebrating their membership in the National Association for the Humor Impaired.

I have received well over a thousand wonderful stories from new found friends all over the United States (as well as Canada, Israel and Australia) and it is impossible to keep track of the source of each story. This book is dedicated to all those who have provided their wonderful stories so that others could share their joy.

In addition to letters received from people who have heard me speak, I have selected limited material from collections of humor published by others. I have included a reference list of the materials that I found particularly entertaining and informative.

INTRODUCTION

This collection of stories is a work of love and the result of a personal journey that began in September of 1987. While reviewing a book on child development I became fascinated with the following quote, "Preschool children laugh or smile on the average of over 400 times per day, while adults over the age of thirty-five only fifteen times per day." I have always enjoyed and appreciated humor but realized I was not very knowledgeable about the subject. I made a personal commitment to spend a half a day a week for a period of three months in libraries and bookstores locating and reviewing material on humor. What began initially as a three month commitment has become a lifelong journey.

In June, 1990, I organized the National Association for the Humor Impaired and currently serve as the Chief Executive Officer (CEO) of the Association. The formation of the Association received national press coverage and because I am a university professor (as well as an attorney) the news articles referred to me as "Dr. Humor," a title that has stuck with me.

The major goal of the Association is to help

the terminally serious to learn to lighten up and enjoy the many benefits of humor. My reading and studying led me to conclude that fifteen percent of the people in America today were humor impaired and another fifteen percent were "at risk" for experiencing humor impairment.

A second goal of the Association is to provide humorous material to prevent the onset of humor impairment, an illness that appears to be reaching epidemic proportions. This book is dedicated to the accomplishment of that goal.

I began reviewing research articles and books on humor from a variety of disciplines such as medicine, education, psychology, sociology, and business management. In addition, my passion for humor led me to read biographies of famous comedians such as Jack Benny, Bob Hope, Joan Rivers, Carol Lawrence, Johnny Carson, Jay Leno, George Burns and David Letterman. I cannot pass a new bookstore without stopping to do a quick review of the material on humor (an obsession which drives my loving family nuts).

I carry a notebook with me everywhere I go and I have learned to look for humor in my daily interactions with others. By looking for humor and asking people I meet to share their favorite stories, I have developed a rich collection of material. For example, recently I was having lunch in the executive lunch room of a large corporation in Minneapolis after I had just delivered a speech on the benefits of humor to 600 employees. I had a brief conversation with the waitress and asked her how she liked her job. She responded, "I like it when I'm kept busy, but when I'm not busy it can be boring and monogamous."

What follows is a collection of joyful stories that I've entitled, "Dear Dr. Humor." A healthy sense of humor is a wonderful gift from God that needs to be exercised daily and shared with others - never leave home without it.

Lastly, I'd like to share the daily prayer of The National Association for the Humor Impaired as a gift to bring you spiritual health and humor:

God, grant me the laughter
to help me see the past with perspective,
to face the future with hope,
and to celebrate today - -
without taking myself too seriously.

Dear Dr. Humor

A Collection of Humorous Stories for All Occasions

Dear Dr. Humor:

When my granddaughter Ann was nine years old she was given an assignment by her teacher to write a story entitled, "Where My Family Came From." The purpose was supposed to be to understand your genealogy.

I was not aware of her assignment when she asked me at the dining room table one night, "Grandma, where did I come from?"

I responded, quite nervously because my son and daughter-in-law were out of town and I was stalling until they returned home.

"Well, honey, the stork brought you."

"Where did Mom come from then?'

"The stork brought her, too."

"Okay, then where did you come from?"

"The stork brought me too, dear."

"Okay, thanks, Grandma."

I did not think anything more about it until two days later when I was cleaning Ann's room and read the first sentence of her paper, "For three generations there have been no natural births in our family."

Dear Dr. Humor:

One night, when our first daughter, Elizabeth, was three years old, a terrible thunder storm frightened her and she climbed in bed with me and my wife. That was fine and we were happy to console her with her fears, but she did the same thing every night between 2 and 4 am for about 4 weeks.

My wife and I consulted a psychologist friend who convinced us that we'd better break the habit, so we made a plan. Every night it happened we put her back in her own bed. It was hard for us because she'd cry and sob, but we stuck to our guns. During the day we'd tell her how proud we were that she was able to stay in her own bed like a big girl.

Right about that time I had to go out of town for three days on a business trip. When I arrived home my wife and daughter met me at O'Hare airport in Chicago. My daughter saw me getting off the plane and ran up to give me a big hug and kiss and yelled very loudly for all to hear, "Daddy, Daddy, I've got some good news, nobody slept with Mommy while you were gone."

Dear Dr. Humor:

Last year our neighbors went on vacation and asked me to check on the house several times while they were away. They left on a Thursday and were to return the following Monday.

On Saturday afternoon, I noticed through the window that our black lab, Boomer, was chewing on something. I went out to see what was in his mouth and was horrified to see it was our neighbors' pet rabbit. Boomer had the poor white rabbit by the neck, it was filthy and very dead. I panicked and felt sick as the neighbor's children were very attached to "Fluffy." I thought that I'd left the neighbors' back door open and that somehow our dog had gotten in the house and killed their rabbit.

I did not know what to do. My husband suggested that we try to locate an identical rabbit from a pet store and replace it so no one would ever know. We spent six hours driving all over Atlanta with "Fluffy" in a freezer bag looking for a rabbit with the same markings, but no success. Finally, we decided to shampoo and blow dry "Fluffy" and return him to his cage to look like he died naturally. We didn't know what else to do.

When our neighbors returned home on Monday, we didn't hear from them. After another day, still no word. I couldn't stand the silence and on the third day I finally called. Jane, our neighbor, told me they had a wonderful time on their vacation but were very puzzled as they found "Fluffy" dead in his cage. I told her I was very sorry to hear that "Fluffy" had died.

She went on to say that the puzzling part was that "Fluffy" had actually died the day before they left and that they had buried him in the backyard.

Dear Dr. Humor:

I graduated from law school in 1981. I had several offers to practice law but none of them were in Nashville, where my family lived and where I wanted to practice law. I decided to borrow money from a bank and open my own office. Law school had prepared me well for law practice but was not very helpful on how to attract clients.

On the second day I was in business, I was arranging my office waiting for my first client. I was sitting idle at my desk when my secretary knocked on my door and told me that a Mr. Simons was here to see me. I responded, "Show him in."

Because I was sensitive to the fact that I did not want my potential client to know that he was my first, I picked up the phone as he was walking in and said: "You tell the insurance company that their offer of $30,000 to settle this case is an insult. We won't consider anything less than $75,000 and I'll give you seven days to get back to me or we're going to trial." I hung up the phone and said, "Mr. Simons, I'm Donald Williamson, how can I help you?"

Mr. Simons responded, "Nice to meet you Mr. Williamson, I'm Alex Simons and I'm here to install your phone."

Dear Dr. Humor:

I want to share a very funny story that happened to me that made me understand how important humor is in our lives and how much it's God's gift that needs to be nurtured.

I am a Lutheran Minister and in April, 1967, I had a very serious car accident and was in the hospital recuperating for seven months. Because I was there so long, I became nonchalant with the nurses and the procedures. You can't keep decorum up for very long with no clothes on. I was also having great difficulty finding a relatively painless spot to put one more injection of pain medication.

I rang for the nurse and when she came on the intercom, I told her I needed another pain shot. I knew exactly how long it would take for her to get there as I'd had lots of practice, so I rolled over in incredible pain so slowly and placed my completely exposed derriere toward the door. I heard her open the door to my room and said, as I pointed to my rear, "You can stick it here."

There was an awful, awful silence. I slowly

struggled to turn over to see a twenty-two year old female parishioner who had come to me. It was particularly awkward because she had flowers and no place to put them. I apologized and tried to chat but she wouldn't come within six feet of me and left shortly thereafter.

Well, thirty seconds after she left, the impact of the situation hit me and I started to laugh. It hurt like you can't imagine, but I laughed and laughed and laughed. Tears were streaming down my face and I was gasping for air when the nurse finally came in. Three times I tried to tell her what had happened, but I couldn't say more than three words without breaking up.

She had to come back three different times before I was calmed down enough to tell her what had happened. By that time I felt absolutely no pain. None. I didn't need medication for nine more hours. It truly was the turning point in my recovery. Also, you'd be interested to know that my parishioner joined another church.

Dear Dr. Humor:

My grandfather told me this story that I thought you would enjoy. My grandfather was a skilled carpenter from Norway who had settled in Northern Wisconsin. In 1950, a wealthy man from Chicago wanted to build a very elaborate hunting lodge in Northern Wisconsin. He contracted with a famous architect in Chicago to design it and the construction company in Northern Wisconsin, for whom my grandfather worked, to build it.

The construction boss received the blue prints and immediately sent a letter to the rich man's house saying, "The plans are all wrong. We can't do nothing until you get them straightened out."

The boss received a letter assuring him that the plans were okay and he should proceed as ordered. By return mail the boss sent the following letter:

"I don't plan to saw a plank until I get the plans straightened out. There is a serious problem. Why, if I was to build that house the way it's laid out on the plans, you'd have two bathrooms."

Dear Dr. Humor:

I have been very successful as an account executive for a medium sized advertising agency. When I first began my employment some 16 years ago, I was very shy and had a very difficult time presenting in front of a group.

My boss suggested that I enroll in a speech class at a local university to improve my skills. I followed his suggestion and I completed an excellent course. One of the techniques the instructor taught us was to focus on one supportive person in the audience who is obviously enjoying your presentation and focus on that person when you speak.

Three weeks after the class was finished, I had to give a presentation to a group of ten people from a local manufacturer. We were competing with three other advertising agencies for the account. I was very nervous and I used the new technique I had learned. One gentlemen was very attentive, smiled and seemed to be genuinely interested in my presentation. By talking to him, I was able to overcome my nervousness and felt the presentation went very well.

   After the presentation we had a short social get together. I went up to the gentleman, thanked him for his attentiveness and support. He then said to me, "Sorry lady, no hablo English."

Dear Dr. Humor:

When I was a graduate student at the University of Nebraska, I worked on a research study involving gifted and talented young children. One of my jobs was to observe and record the verbal interactions between young children and their parents.

While collecting my data, the following conversation took place between a five-year-old gifted child and his father.

Child: "Daddy, what is electricity?"

Father: "I really don't know, but it makes things run."

Child: "Daddy, how does gasoline make the car run?"

Father: "Billy, I don't know much about gasoline engines."

Child: "Daddy, I hope you don't mind me asking all these questions."

Father: "Not at all, son. It's important that you keep asking for how else will you ever learn anything?"

Dear Dr. Humor:

I am a kindergarten teacher. Several years ago, I got on a bus and sat down next to a man who looked familiar. Smiling pleasantly I turned and talked to him. He was awkward and didn't respond well. I then realized that he was not someone that I knew.

Feeling kind of awkward, I said, "Oh, excuse me. I mistook you for someone else. I thought you were the father of two of my children." Before I realized what I had said, he got up and moved to a different seat. I couldn't wait to get off that bus.

Dear Dr. Humor:

I remember years ago viewing Art Linkletter as he conducted an interview with a little girl on his television show "House Party." I believe the little girl's name was Julie and she was five-years-old. The following exchange took place:

Mr. Linkletter:	"Do you have any pets?"
Julie:	"No, I did have a fish but he died."
Mr. Linkletter:	"And it went to fish heaven?"
Julie:	"No, I flushed him down the toilet."

Dear Dr. Humor:

When our daughter Mary was celebrating her 9th birthday, we decided to invite her friends and their parents for a dinner party. We invited four children and eight adults.

Earlier in the day, Mary had opened her presents from the family and was so pleased to receive, among others, the two gifts she really wanted - a watch and bottle of expensive perfume. She chattered all day long about the two gifts to the point where it was driving the whole family crazy.

Before the guests arrived for the party I told Mary nicely that she shouldn't babble on all night about her gifts. Throughout the dinner she kept fairly quiet until finally she couldn't stand it any more and said, "If anyone hears anything or smells anything, it's me."

Dear Dr. Humor:

My sister teaches first grade in Chicago. Toward the end of the school year, the class went on à field trip to the Museum of Natural History. All 28 students had a full day and my sister was exhausted when she got home.

She was in the bathtub soaking when the phone rang. It was a parent who was laughing hysterically. The parent had asked her son how he enjoyed the field trip and the boy said, "It was great. We should take the whole family to the dead circus."

Dear Dr. Humor:

My mother tells the following story which took place when she was a third grader enrolled in a county school in Nebraska. There had been a big snowstorm and the teacher warned the students about playing too long in the snow.

The teacher told them that when she was a child she had a seven year old brother who went out with a new sled, played for too many hours and caught cold, pneumonia had set in and he died three days later. The classroom was very quiet and then a youngster raised his hand and asked, "Where's his sled?"

Dear Dr. Humor:

We moved from Chicago to Florida for retirement three years ago. We purchased a house with four acres, which was a great deal more land than we had had in Chicago. We decided to grow a large garden in order to sell the vegetables and supplement our income. It got so large that we had to hire a gardener to help.

After two months my husband caught the gardener stealing vegetables, selling them and pocketing the money. My husband fired him on the spot. Two weeks later we got a request for a reference for the gardener for another job. My husband and I thought, "Of all the gall."

We thought about it and decided to have some fun. My husband and I composed the following letter: "Mike Smith, our former gardener, got more out of my garden than any gardener I've ever known."

Dear Dr. Humor:

In 1987, my uncle lost his wife to cancer. They loved each other very much and he was very depressed for about a year following her death. On her tombstone he had engraved the line, "My light has gone out."

Three years later he met a woman whom he fell in love with and decided to marry. About three weeks prior to his marriage he talked with his local pastor as to whether he should have the tombstone replaced with something more appropriate now that he was remarrying.

Since my uncle was not wealthy, the pastor suggested rather than replacing the old tombstone he simply have it modified to read, "But I have struck another match."

Dear Dr. Humor:

Last year my wife and I attended a funeral. It was the funeral of the husband of a lady who works with my wife in an insurance office. Neither of us really knew the deceased well and we attended the funeral out of respect to the widow.

During the service the minister got a little carried away. At the end of his comments about what a wonderful person the deceased was, he followed up with "It is important for the living to remember that, although the body leaves us, the soul remains..... although the shell is gone, the nut remains."

I had all I could do to control myself from erupting with laughter.

Dear Dr. Humor:

I gave a speech about quality improvement at a business management convention. I worked for several months preparing the presentation and truly felt that I had done a very good job.

After I finished and received strong applause from the members of the audience, a number of people came up afterward to ask questions and to tell me how pleased they were with my presentation. I was feeling very good about the feedback I was receiving.

Then a very nice gentleman came up to me and said in all sincerity, "You'll never know what your presentation meant to me. It was just like water to a drowning man."

Dear Dr. Humor:

I have worked for the same insurance company for 17 years. I have had a variety of jobs, but one of the most interesting was to review and investigate claims of injury or death. Once in a while in reviewing the claim forms you run across some light-hearted material.

One claim form for $50,000 of life insurance described how a farmer who was roofing his barn, lost his balance, fell and broke his neck. At the bottom of the form there is a section simply labeled "remarks." The farmer's widow responded, "He didn't make none."

Dear Dr. Humor:

I work as a bank teller at a busy drive-up window in Long Beach, California. There are two funny incidents that I'd like to share:

A young lady, whom I did not recognize as a regular customer, asked me if I could cash a two party check for her. I said to her, "I'm sure the check is all right, but could you show me some positive identification?"

She thought for a second, turned her face sideways and said, "I have a mole just above my right ear."

The second incident happened when I was working on a very windy day. Throughout the day, customers would place their paperwork in the drawer and the wind would blow it away before I was able to close the drawer. I got a paper weight and put in the drawer.

I instructed the next customer, an attractively dressed lady, to, "Put the weight on the check." When I received the check, under the customer's name was written "128 pounds."

Dear Dr. Humor:

This story didn't actually happen to me, but I read it in a New York newspaper several years ago. There was an article about a group of four gang members in New York who robbed all the commuters on a subway car. The gang members stole money, credit cards, jewels and other valuables from the passengers.

One man who was about to be separated from all his valuables, pulled a twenty dollar bill out of his pocket, gave it to his friend sitting next to him and said, "Here, Mike, here's the $20 I owe you."

Dear Dr. Humor:

I work as an attorney for the District Attorney's Office in the Bronx. On one of my cases, a nervous young lawyer came forward when his client's case was called. He laid his hat and coat on the bench where the observers sit and stood before the Judge.

The Judge said to him, "Is this the first time you've practiced in this Court?" "Yes, your Honor," responded the attorney, feeling somewhat awkward and nervous. The Judge then said, "I could tell because no experienced lawyer in my court would leave their hat and coat in a place where you can't keep an eye on them."

Dear Dr. Humor:

I am an elementary school teacher from Joplin, Missouri. Last year I received a traffic ticket for going through a red light in town. I truly felt that the officer was wrong and I decided to fight the ticket.

On the day I was to appear in court there were three other cases scheduled. I explained to the judge that I was a third grade teacher and requested that he hear my case first so that I could get to school. The Judge granted my wish, chose to believe the policeman's version and found me guilty.

Regarding my fine the Judge stated, "Madam, today, I shall realize my lifelong wish. I've waited years to have a school teacher in my court room. You are to sit down at that table and write 500 times, 'I will never go through a red light again.' "

Dear Dr. Humor:

My husband is a pilot for one of the major airlines which prides itself on being on time. Last December, as a result of minor repairs, his flight was an hour late leaving Minneapolis for Los Angeles.

After the plane was up in the air about 45 minutes my husband announced to the passengers:

"Ladies and gentlemen, I want to apologize for our delay in leaving Minneapolis. You see, the machine that normally rips the handles off your luggage was broken today. We had to do it by hand."

My husband received many comments from the passengers that they enjoyed his sense of humor. Unfortunately, there was a vice president. from the airline on the flight and my husband was suspended for two weeks.

Dear Dr. Humor:

As a surprise birthday present to my lovely bride of 22 years, I arranged to have a college student come in once a week to clean the house. My wife loved the idea and was very appreciative.

Carol, the student, was to clean the house each Thursday from 10 to 12. For the first two weeks my wife arranged her work schedule so she could show Carol exactly what and how she wanted the house cleaned. In addition, my wife and Carol had agreed that my wife would leave a list on the dishwasher of any additional things that needed to be done. The list the third week included: 1. Dust the living room furniture and 2. Shake the throw rugs in the dining room.

I had forgotten my briefcase at home and went home just before noon to pick it up. Carol greeted me and said she had just vacuumed the whole house and all she had left to do was the two additional tasks on my wife's list. As I was about to leave for the office, I noticed that she was literally following my wife's request. I could hardly believe my eyes but there she was, standing in the dining room, shaking the dirty throw rugs!

Dear Dr. Humor:

Deb, a friend of mine, was standing beside her sister at their mother's funeral. They were standing in a receiving line to greet guests attending the funeral. One lady commented to Deb that her sister was a "dead ringer" for their mother.

Deb's sister didn't hear the comment, so Deb, who has a great sense of humor and was able to keep her composure, said, "You may want to rephrase that!"

Dear Dr. Humor:

My brother works for a telemarketing firm that sells products by phone. One day he called a home phone and the phone was answered by a small boy in a whisper. All of the boy's responses were whispered in the following conversation:

Q: "Is your father home?"

A: "Yes."

Q: "May I speak to him?"

A: "No."

Q: "Is your mother home?"

A: "Yes."

Q: "May I speak to her?"

A: "No."

Q: "Is there anyone else there?"

A: "Yes."

Q: "Who else is there?"

A: "A policeman."

Q: "Who else is there?"

A: "Two firemen."

Q: "What are they doing?"

A: "Looking for me!"

Dear Dr. Humor:

A business partner called my house on a Saturday. Bobby, my twelve-year-old son was babysitting my daughter, Danielle, who was four at the time. Bobby was out in the backyard when my partner called and Danielle answered the phone. My partner told me about the following phone conversation:

A: "Hello."

Q: "Hello, is your father home?"

A: "I'm sorry, no one is here. Can I take a message?"

Q: "Yes, please tell your father that Mr. Brown called."

A: "Just a minute please."

After a very long pause, Danielle said "O.K., I'm ready."

"Who is this did you say?"

A: "Mr. Brown."

Q: "How do you spell Brown?"

A: "B-r-o-w-n."

Q: (after a long pause) "How do you make a B?"

Dear Dr. Humor:

Christmas at Grandpa and Grandma's was always a large gathering of 13 kids and lots of grand kids. This particular year, the presents that Grandma had bought for the offspring were unusually large and bulky - much too big to put under the tree. Grandpa got the idea of hiding the presents all over the house and giving everyone the first clue to a treasure hunt to find their presents.

Then Grandpa surprised Grandma giving her a clue to find her present. It read, "First Book 18th Chapter, 21st Verse."

That verse in Genesis mentions firewood, where Grandpa had hidden the present. However, in her excitement and haste, Grandma mistakenly read the 19th Chapter, 21st verse. There she read, "And Sarah laughed, shall I give Abraham a son in his old age?"

Dear Dr. Humor:

We have three daughters and two years ago, the youngest one, who had just turned two, wandered into the house with a horrified look on her face - it looked as if she was going to spit something. I grabbed a napkin and as she spit what was in her mouth I realized that it smelled like, and was, dog feces. I rinsed her mouth out and refrained from kissing her for a while.

A year later when our oldest daughter, who was a second grader, was receiving First Communion, our priest was talking to all the parents and children as a group and asked if there was anything that they'd like to pray about. Our second daughter who was four years old said loudly for all in the room to hear, "One time, Kelsey ate a dog turd". It brought the house down.

Dear Dr. Humor:

I saved the attached article. It was a book review of "Lady Chatterly's Lover" that was published in, of all places, *Field and Stream Magazine* (Nov. 1959 issue):

"Although written many years ago, "Lady Chatterly's Lover" has just been reissued by Grove Press, and this fictional account of the day-by-day life of an English gamekeeper is still of considerable interest to outdoor-minded readers, as it contains many passages on pheasant raising, the apprehending of poachers, ways to control vermin, and other chores and duties of the professional gamekeeper. Unfortunately one is obliged to wade through many pages of extraneous materials in order to discover and savor these sidelights on the management of a Midlands shooting estate, and in this reviewer's opinion this book cannot take the place of J.R. Miller's "Practical Gamekeeping.""

Dear Dr. Humor:

My wife and I were at a local restaurant for lunch when we overheard a conversation between the people sitting at the next table. A mother, father and young child were seated by the hostess.

After the waitress had gotten the parents' order she approached the young child who looked to be around five years old and said, "And what can I get for you?"
The boy responded, "I'd like a hot dog, and..."
"No, no," the mother interrupted, "no hot dogs. He'll have the hot turkey sandwich, mashed potatoes, no gravy, and skim milk."
But the waitress ignored the mother and asked the boy directly, "Ketchup or mustard on your hot dog?"
"Ketchup and a coke, please," replied the boy.
The waitress started for the kitchen and said, "Coming up!"
The young boy said to his parents, "Know what? She thinks I'm real."

Dear Dr. Humor:

I read this story about neighbors in our hometown newspaper. The Schmidts and the Andersons live next to each other on the block behind my house. Apparently they don't get along very well.

Anyway, Mr. Anderson received a phone call at 2:30 am from Mr. Schmidt. Schmidt woke Anderson up and when Anderson picked up the phone Schmidt simply said in an angry tone, "Anderson, your dog is barking and keeping me awake all night," and then hung up before there was a chance to reply.

Two nights later at 3:00 am, Anderson returned a phone call to Schmidt. When Schmidt picked up the phone Anderson said simply, "Schmidt, I don't have a dog."

Dear Dr. Humor:

One morning my husband and I were having breakfast with our 20-year-old daughter. Our daughter was telling us about her date from the previous night. She told us how they had driven to another city for dinner and a movie. When my husband asked her where the restaurant was located, she said, "I really don't know as I was enjoying the ride, the company and the scenery, and all of a sudden we were there."

My husband then said, "I understand completely. That's exactly how your mother and I arrived at middle age."

Dear Dr. Humor:

You asked members to send you their favorite stories. I remember a wonderful story that happened in New York City in 1982. There was this small hotel that was purchased by a large corporation. The corporation invested 3 million dollars to give the hotel a facelift and then began to focus on promotion. They hired a slick promotion company that designed a total program to promote the hotel.

One of the promotion strategies was to go after vacation travelers. They developed a mailing list of all the husband and wife guests who had stayed in the hotel over the past three years and sent them a letter acknowledging their past business and a free Valentine card with a coupon for a free night's stay to see the new refurbishment.

As a result of the promotion, there were 11 divorces and the hotel manager was subpoenaed to testify in six of the divorce trials.

Dear Dr. Humor:

My wife and I were having dinner with some friends at a fancy restaurant in Buffalo, New York. My wife loves prime rib well done and detests it when it's pink or rare. When she ordered her prime rib she told the waiter, "You can't over cook it for my tastes. Please stress to the cook 'well done'."

We all were served our meal and when my wife cut into her prime rib, even though it looked well done on the outside, it was very rare.

My wife was a little irritated, so when the waiter returned I said to him, "Didn't you hear my wife say 'well done'?" The waiter responded to my wife, "Thank you very much, madam. I hardly ever get a compliment."

Dear Dr. Humor:

I am an executive secretary for a large investment company on Wall Street. Last year, the boss took four of us out for a delicious, but large, lunch for secretary's day. During lunch, my boss teased me about burning off the calories from the lunch, as he knows that I am an avid jogger and that I work out everyday after work.

Our boss, who had also enjoyed the good food, suggested toward the end of the day, as I was getting ready to go home, that I run an extra lap for him.

Walking out the door, with important clients in the waiting room, I said to the boss, "Get ready to start huffing and puffing because I'll be on your lap in half an hour." When I realized what I'd said, I wanted to crawl out of the office.

Dear Dr. Humor:

My father-in-law had gained a lot of weight when he gave up smoking. One evening my wife and I were at my in-laws' home watching TV when my father-in-law inadvertently stepped in front of the TV screen. My mother-in-law got a wistful look in her eye as she said, "I remember when he covered only half the screen."

Dear Dr. Humor:

I am principal of a public high school in a small town in Minnesota. Last year at the end of the school year, a student by the name of Jimmy Sechauer (pronounced sex hour) told me that he would not be attending my school next year as he was moving to a new house in a neighboring district.

Two weeks into the next fall term, I realized that the neighboring district had not requested Jimmy's school records, which is standard procedure for a transfer student. I called the neighboring high school and the secretary answered the phone. I said, "Do you have a Sechauer over there?" She responded, "Hell no, we don't even get a coffee break."

Dear Dr. Humor:

I am a university professor in education. Often at conventions you run into past graduates and it is very embarrassing when you can't recall their names. I attended a convention several years ago and as I was conversing with a fellow professor, I noticed out of the corner of my eye a former student who was approaching.

I was racking my brain to try and recall his name, and finally it came to me. I turned to him and said "Hi, Fred, How are you doing?" I further said, "Fred Peepers, I'd like you to meet Dr. Williams." He responded, "Nice to meet you Dr. Williams, my name is Fred Flasher."

Dear Dr. Humor:

I read this story in Reader's Digest and liked it so much I cut it out and saved it for years.

For his wife's birthday party, my doctor ordered a cake with this inscription: "You Are Not Getting Older, You Are Just Getting Better." Asked how he wanted the message arranged, he told the baker, "Just put 'You Are Not Getting Older' at the top and 'You Are Just Getting Better' at the bottom."

It wasn't until the doctor was ready to serve the cake that he discovered it read, "You Are Not Getting Older at the Top, You Are Just Getting Better at the Bottom."

Dear Dr. Humor:

I am an attorney who practices divorce law. One day I was waiting to enter the courtroom with my client when the doors opened and an angry woman came out. She shouted, "I hate lawyers!" She then turned to her attorney and said, "Even though you're my lawyer, I'm sorry, but I hate lawyers." She went on to say, "My ex-husband is a lawyer and I hate him. Oh, I'm getting married again, all right, but you'd better believe that it won't be another lawyer. Maybe I'll marry a doctor."

With that, my client tapped the woman on the shoulder and said, "If you wait here for ten minutes, there will be a doctor available."

Dear Dr. Humor:

I was out of town and my wife, a high-school teacher, had to contend with a furnace that went out in the middle of the night. Fortunately, a 24 hour repairman arrived that evening and worked until the early morning hours. The next day my tired wife was late for school. She hastily wrote an explanation for the vice principal and rushed to her class.

Five minutes later the vice principal burst into her classroom, laughing, and asked if she would like to reword her note. My wife had written: "Husband out of town. No heat. Up all night with repairman. Totally exhausted."

Dear Dr. Humor:

I worked during college as a waiter at a large resort in the Catskill Mountains. Usually, the guests sat at the same tables for all their meals and waiters were assigned to specific tables. One of the guests was a wealthy man who was very generous with his tipping.

Midway through the week I started waiting the table where the big tipper sat with his family. The first thing he asked me was, "Where is Brian, our regular waiter?"

I answered honestly, "My name's Steve. Brian won't be your waiter anymore because I won you in a poker game last night."

Dear Dr. Humor:

New neighbors moved in next door to us several years ago. I hadn't met them yet but I noticed that they seemed to be a very affectionate couple. I said to my husband at breakfast one morning, "The new neighbors seem like a very devoted couple. Every time the husband leaves for work she comes out on the porch and he hugs and kisses her. Why don't you do that?"

"Me?" my husband responded, "I should say not. I haven't even been introduced to her yet."

Dear Dr. Humor:

I teach Sunday School at our Lutheran Church in a small town in Minnesota. Billy, a cute little second grader, had been absent for several Sundays in a row. When he arrived one Sunday, I said to him, "I'm so glad you came today, we've missed you."

Billy said, "Well, I almost didn't make it. I started to go fishing but my father wouldn't let me."

I responded, "I'm glad your father wouldn't let you go fishing on Sunday. And I hope he told you the reason. Did he?"

"Yes," said Billy, "Dad said he didn't have enough worms for both of us."

Dear Dr. Humor:

We were a host family for a foreign exchange student from Columbia. Hector was a wonderful young man but his English was not very good when he first arrived.

My wife loves flowers and plants and our home is always overflowing with both. One day Hector noticed a new plant in the sun porch and asked my wife what kind of plant it was, as he would like to take such a plant back home to his mother.

My wife responded that, "It belongs to the begonia family." Hector was quiet for a moment and then said, "Do you think the Begonias would know what kind of plant it is?"

Dear Dr. Humor:

My husband was appointed superintendent of a state mental hospital. He had worked for many years as an assistant superintendent and we were very excited about his promotion. His first day on the job, a mental patient said to him, "I like you a lot better than our last superintendent."

My husband said to him, "And why is that?" To which the gentleman responded, "Somehow you just seem like one of us."

Dear Dr. Humor:

My husband and I had just bought our first home and we were thrilled with it. It was a great house and a great neighborhood. After we had been in the house a week, I wanted to get to know our neighbors and I invited the lady next door for coffee.

We were visiting at the kitchen table and getting acquainted. I asked her what her husband did for a living. She told me that he was an expediter for an air conditioning manufacturer. She must have noticed the quizzical look on my face as she asked, "Do you know what an expediter does?" To which I responded, "No."

"That's O.K.," she said, "I didn't know what it was either until my husband took the job. The best way I can describe it is that if we women did what he does, they'd call it nagging."

Dear Dr. Humor:

The following letter I found in Eric Johnson's 1991 book, "Humorous Stories About the Human Condition." It's a great book and I would highly recommend it to you. A Mr. Ted Andrews had written to a rural motel to inquire whether his dog would be able to stay there. He received the following reply:

Dear Mr. Andrews:

I have been in the motel business for over twenty years. Never yet have I had to call in the police to eject a disorderly dog in the wee hours of the morning. No dog has ever attempted to pass off a bad check on me. Never has a dog set the bedclothes afire through smoking. I have never found hotel towels in a dog's suitcase. Your dog is welcome.

P.S. If he will vouch for you, you can come, too.

Dear Dr. Humor:

My sister-in-law had been married seven years. She and her husband had been trying to conceive a child. She finally ended up going to a fertility clinic. After a two hour examination and a lot of tests, she was asked to sit in the waiting room. After another hour, a nurse called her name to come into the doctor's office to review what he had found.

He explained in great detail the results of each of the tests and what they meant and concluded by saying, "I think I can get you pregnant." She immediately responded, "I had hoped my husband would do that part."

Dear Dr. Humor:

I was working as a teacher's assistant at a preschool program. We took all the kids on a field trip to a large nursery and florist shop. Children can sometimes be so honest and blunt that it takes you back a few paces once in a while.

I was with our group of 23 students when we arrived by bus at the nursery. A very nice elderly woman greeted us as we exited the bus and the following exchange took place between the woman and Sara, one of the children.

The Lady said to Sara, "How do you do, my dear?" "Fine, thank you," replied the girl. There was a pause and then the lady said, "Why don't you ask me how I am?"

"Because," replied the girl in a pleasant tone, "I'm not interested."

Dear Dr. Humor:

One of the first jobs I had as a doctor was with a medical clinic that served the needs of the elderly in their homes in a poor section of West Virginia. One of my first patients commented when I arrived at his house, "Doctor, I sure am glad to meet you and I appreciate your coming to the house. But isn't it pretty far out of your way to visit here?"

I responded, "It's not too bad, I have another patient right down the road so I'm able to kill two birds with one stone." The patient responded, "I sure wish you'd say it a little different, Doc."

Dear Dr. Humor:

When I was 15 years old I was having a serious conversation with my grandmother, whom I adored. I asked grandma, "What kind of husband do you think I should look for?"

My grandmother answered, "You just leave husbands alone and you find yourself a nice, single fellow."

Dear Dr. Humor:

When I was in college I had the same boyfriend for three years. We met when I was a freshman and he was a senior. When he graduated, he took a job in Boston and I remained in Salt Lake City. He knew how much I loved fresh seafood and each time he flew to Salt Lake City to be with me, he would bring a box of fresh packed crabs and lobster.

On one occasion, as he boarded the plane in Boston, the flight attendant told him that the box was too big to fit in the overhead bin and that she would store it in the back of the plane for him. Shortly after the pilot announced that the plane was making an approach to land in Salt Lake City, the flight attendant came on the intercom and said, "Would the gentleman who gave me the crabs please ring his call button." My boyfriend was too embarrassed to push the call button and the attendant, after having realized what she said, was almost hysterical, as were many of the passengers.

Dear Dr. Humor:

My aunt took a Caribbean cruise three years ago. She booked her cabin as a single and was hopeful to meet a desirable single man. She liked everything about the cruise except the seating arrangements in the dining room, where she was seated at a table with women only.

On the second day out, she met the captain and said to him, "Everything about the cruise is wonderful except that I'm at a table with women only. Would it be possible for you to put me at a table with some nice bachelors?" The captain said he would try to arrange it.

That evening, when she went to dinner, she discovered that the captain had moved her to another table. This time she was seated with seven young priests.

Dear Dr. Humor:

I've been employed as a telephone operator for thirteen years. I had a number of funny things happen to me over the years, but my favorite happened about three years ago. A customer had been trying to call his home for over an hour and kept getting a busy signal. Finally he called me and asked if I could cut in on the line. I told him that I could only cut in a phone conversation if it was an emergency, or a case of life or death.

The man responded, "Well, I can tell you this much, if it's my teenage daughter on the phone, there's going to be a murder."

Dear Dr. Humor:

I attended a Rotary meeting several years ago and the speaker, whose topic was, "How to Deal With Stress in the 90's" gave a tremendous speech and received a standing ovation. The President of the Rotary Club was so impressed that he said to the speaker, "Everyone was so enthused about your presentation, I wonder if you wouldn't consider saying a few more words since we have about ten minutes left?"

The speaker stood up, walked to the podium, and said, "Once upon a time there was a little cabbage who said to his mother, 'Mommy, I'm worried about something. As I sit in this row of cabbages and grow and grow and grow day after day, how will I know when to stop growing?' 'The rule to follow,' the mamma cabbage said, 'is to quit when you are a head.'" Then he sat down.

Dear Dr. Humor:

While in the Navy, I was stationed in the Mediterranean for nine months. One leave, myself and three of my fellow sailors decided to travel for two weeks through the Scandinavian countries. While we were in Norway, we decided to go to church on Sunday morning. Not understanding Norwegian, we were not exactly sure what to do so we decided to simply followed the gentleman sitting in the pew in front of us.

During the service the minister made a special announcement and the man in front of us stood up. All four of us sailors followed him and rose to our feet. Immediately there was a loud roar of laughter from the whole congregation. We were embarrassed and confused.

When the service was over we were greeted by the minister at the door and we discovered that he spoke English. He explained to us, still laughing, that he had announced a baptism for next week and asked that the father of the child please rise.

Dear Dr. Humor:

As a minister, I was assigned to a new parish in Nebraska in 1972. Before I arrived, the parish had just finished a major building program, and in addition to a new church, there was a beautiful adjoining elementary school with eight classrooms.

Following the first church service, we hosted an open house in the new school. As we were touring the school, a seven-year-old girl said, "It certainly is a beautiful building. Who was the artichoke who designed it?"

Dear Dr. Humor:

My husband is a cardiologist and is on the staff of a major hospital in New York. One night he came home and was completely exhausted from several long days in a row. He planned to go to bed around eight o'clock to get a good night's sleep. No sooner had he gotten in bed than the phone rang. He told me to find out who it was and to say that he wouldn't be home until much later.

I said to the person on the phone, "I'm sorry, but the doctor is not at home."

"Well," the voice said, "I'm one of his patients. I've got a sudden chest pain and I want to see him as soon as I can."

My husband was listening to the phone conversation and whispered some instructions to me to pass on to the caller. At the end I said, "Do that and I'm sure you'll soon feel better."

"Thanks very much," the lady said, "but tell me, is that person with you qualified to give medical advice?"

Dear Dr. Humor:

My wife is a pharmaceutical sales representative for a major drug company. She has a large territory and is gone overnight on an average of ten nights a month. She was staying at a hotel in Cincinnati and was totally exhausted. She went down to the dining room, looked at the menu and said to the waiter, "Just bring me a good dinner, I don't care what it is."

The waiter brought her a delicious prime rib dinner with all the extras. When she paid the bill she gave him a large tip and thanked him. The waiter said, "It was a pleasure serving you, and if you have any friends who can't read either, just tell them to ask for Fred as their waiter."

Dear Dr. Humor:

I sometimes worry about retiring and staying home all day with my wife. Don't get me wrong, I love my wife dearly but we've both talked about the potential difficulties that would arise if I were home full time. As the saying goes, "For better or worse, but not for lunch."

I had a small taste of what it might be like several months ago when my wife was quite ill with the flu. I stayed home for two days to help her. I was trying to fix breakfast and I called to her, "I can't find the tea bags, dear."

She answered, "They are right on the first shelf, in a coffee can marked 'rice'."

Dear Dr. Humor:

My sister and I were traveling throughout Europe and Africa two summers ago. My sister is a dear soul but every time we were staying in less than a five star hotel, she was insistent that we locate the fire escape even before we unpacked our clothes. Our hotel in Cairo was not the greatest and as soon as we opened the door to our room on the seventh floor, my sister went exploring to locate the fire escape.

She was having trouble locating it when she opened an unmarked door to find it was a bathroom in which a heavy set man was in the bath tub. My sister was very embarrassed and said, "I'm so very sorry, I was looking for the fire escape."

As she tried to hurry back to her room, the man followed her, barefoot and dripping wet with a towel around him, he yelled, "Wait for me, lady, I don't want to burn to death."

Dear Dr. Humor:

I was let go from my job because the company was in financial difficulty and I was able to find a comparable job with a company located 120 miles away. Rather than commute daily, I often stayed overnight during the week and then joined my wife for the weekend.

Once, my wife decided to surprise me. She telephoned the motel where I always stayed and asked the desk clerk to tell me that she was coming to spend the night with me. She was sure that she would arrive in time for dinner.

As it turned out we both arrived at the motel at 5 pm. After kissing and hugging, we walked into the lobby of the motel arm in arm. The desk clerk ran up to me and asked if he could talk to me privately. He then said, "Get rid of that woman. Your wife is on the way."

Dear Dr. Humor:

In 1989, my wife and I had a lovely vacation traveling through Britain. Two days before we were to leave, my wife became violently ill and we had to see the doctor. My wife responded very well to the medication the doctor prescribed and we were able to go on the trip. When we returned home she received the following note from her best friend:

"Your daughter tells me that you hadn't been feeling well, and that your husband took you to London and Edinburgh. Please tell him that I'm not feeling so hot and that I've never been to Switzerland."

Dear Dr. Humor:

When my husband and I had our first child, Elizabeth, we were very conscientious about being parents and wanted to do a first rate job. We obtained our first baby sitter when Elizabeth was 18 months old. We received several recommendations from neighbors and selected a sitter that we felt was responsible and had lots of experience with young children.

When we returned home at 10 pm we were very upset to find Elizabeth still wide awake in the family room and the sitter on the phone chatting away with a friend. We also noticed that a full bottle of Tums was open and half empty. The sitter told us that Elizabeth had eaten half the bottle before she noticed it.

I panicked and called my pediatrician right away. I told him that Elizabeth had just eaten a half a bottle of Tums and wanted to know if I should take her to the hospital emergency room to have her stomach pumped. My doctor thought for a moment and said, "If it were my daughter, I'd take her out for Mexican food."

Dear Dr. Humor:

I was breastfeeding our third child when our inquisitive four-year-old came up to me and asked what I was doing. I explained that I was breastfeeding the baby. He asked, "What is in there?" To which I responded, "The baby's milk." After a pause, he asked, "Is there orange juice in the other one?"

Dear Dr. Humor:

We were invited to the wedding of a wonderful gal who had been our babysitter for three years. My five year old son, Mark, was very attached to her and so excited to receive the invitation. He had never been to a wedding before and was asking me all kinds of questions. Finally, he wanted to know, "Do we get to go to the conception afterward?"

Dear Dr. Humor:

When my son was 3 years old we enjoyed biking and he was in the carrier on the back of my bike. Often we would bike through the local cemetery to avoid traffic. One day my son said to me, "Mom, I know what happens to people when they die. You plant them in the ground and they grow up to be statues."

Dear Dr. Humor:

When my son was four years old, he had the opportunity to watch "101 Dalmatians." Several days later when we were traveling to visit my parents who live in the country, we passed a field in which there was a large herd of cows and Danny said, "Look Mom, dalmatian cows."

Dear Dr. Humor

I remember when my father-in-law was in the hospital for a very delicate brain operation; he had some post-operative infections and was in intensive care, near death (Fortunately, he lived). On one of the times that he came to, the nurse said to him, "Sir, do you know what state you're in?"

My father-in-law looked at her, with this befuddled look on his face, and said, "Confusion?" Although it was a very tense situation, my father-in-law's answer had us all in stitches.

Dear Dr. Humor:

In the early years of our marriage, my brother-in-law gave us a turkey he had won bowling. My husband and I felt the turkey was too large for us to cook for one dinner, so I decided to take it to the neighborhood butcher to have the turkey cut in half. My husband was using the car, so I decided to walk the block to the store. The turkey was frozen solid. I grabbed a baby blanket and wrapped the turkey up and headed off to the store.

At the store, this precious, sweet little old lady walked up to me and ohhhed and ahhhed over my 'baby' and asked to see her. I was at a loss for words and didn't want to embarrass her. I stammered and stuttered and finally mumbled something like, "the baby was cold and I didn't want to unwrap her."

The sweet lady just smiled and said she understood. Then she said she could see the baby's darling bald head and just knew how adorable the baby must be. I waited at the back of the store, smiling and holding my 'baby', until I saw the lady finish at the checkout counter and leave the store before taking my baby to the butcher to be cut in half.

Dear Dr. Humor:

One time when I was taking care of my grand-daughters, they were riding in the back seat, and Brianna said, "We aren't supposed to say the F word." And I thought, "Uh-oh." Christian piped up and said, "No, we're supposed to say gas." I laughed so hard I had to stop the car, get out and walk around and pretend I was checking the tires.

Dear Dr. Humor:

When I was 19, I worked at Disney World in Florida driving the submarines in 20,000 Leagues Under the Sea. The submarines traveled on a track, and on busy days the submarines in the back would be held up in a given area while the submarines up front were loading and unloading passengers. Invariably, we would be stuck in what we called the Octopus Section, which was a scene showing an octopus guarding treasure. People would wonder why we were stopped.

I was instructed to get on the microphone and say, "Ladies and gentlemen, there has been a slight delay. Apparently, one of the octopus' tentacles has been wrapped up in a propeller. We're sending divers to straighten it out."

But one time, I don't know what I was thinking, because I said, "Ladies and gentlemen, there is going to be a slight delay. Apparently, one of the octopus' testicles is wrapped up in our propeller." Nobody laughed, and then I realized what I had said. I was so embarrassed that I couldn't show my face as people were unloading.

Dear Dr. Humor:

Several years ago, I attended a funeral for a wonderful woman who'd died very unexpectedly. The church was full to its capacity with people who had come to pay their respects. It was at a time when the song 'Wind Beneath My Wings' was popular, and it was selected as a song to be played during the funeral. The song was to be played after the oldest grandson had delivered the eulogy. It was a very tense moment as the grandson was unable to finish because he was very emotional.

The time for the music came and whoever was operating the record player dropped the needle on the wrong spot. The church was filled with 'Under the Boardwalk.' People had been crying so hard before, during the eulogy, that it went immediately to tears of laughter.

Dear Dr. Humor:

Every Saturday I visit my mother-in-law in a local nursing home. I take her to lunch at noon and stay with her while she eats. She sits at the dining room table with three other ladies. One Saturday one of the nurses was having great difficulty in giving a patient her medication. The patient was moaning and groaning that she didn't need it.

Bernice, who is in her 90's and sits at the same table as my mother-in-law, was taking this all in. She looked at me and in a serious tone said, "Aren't all these old people annoying." I couldn't help but chuckle to myself.

Dear Dr. Humor:

I am a nurse who works in the emergency room at a large city hospital. A lady came into the emergency room with a broken arm. When I asked her how she injured herself, she told me exactly what had happened (I would have lied through my teeth - the story would have remained with me until my funeral).

Due to her honesty, the emergency room medical records state that she "fell off her bedroom dresser while attempting to bend over in order to see her hemorrhoids in the dresser mirror."

Dear Dr. Humor:

As a pediatric nurse, I frequently have an opportunity to observe children at play. Some children, because of their chronic disease, become very hospital-wise. On one occasion, I was watching two 8 year old boys at play. One boy, who was very hospital-wise, asked the second boy, "Are you a medical patient or a surgical patient?" The second little boy responded, "I don't know." The first little boy looked at him seriously and said, "Well, were you sick when you came in here or did they make you sick after you got here?"

Dear Dr. Humor:

My wife and I were taking our grandson to church, and we had to go by a local prison. As we went by, my grandson said to me, "Grandpa, they have a lot of bad people in there."

I responded by saying, "I hope they learn to behave." My grandson was quiet for a while and then he was ready to respond. (A point of information is that my grandson is often disciplined by having him sit on a couch.) He said, "Grandpa, I bet they have a lot of couches in there."

Dear Dr. Humor:

When I was a junior in high school I had a crush on this senior dreamboat. I didn't think he even knew who I was until one night he called me at home and asked me out for the following night. Needless to say I was very excited, I so much wanted to make a positive impression on him.

We were to go out for dinner and then to a movie. I looked like a million dollars and felt very confident when he came to the door to pick me up. After he met my parents we left for our date. Like the prince of my dreams, he opened the car door for me and I slid into the passenger seat. At the same time, probably because I was so nervous, I had to pass gas. As soon as he closed the door, I let out the gas with a loud noise. I was sure he did not hear. When he got in the car he turned to me and gesturing to the back seat said, "I'd like to introduce you to Jim and Kate, the folks we're doubling with."

Dear Dr. Humor:

I used to work at a day care. The owner of the day care lived on the premises with her husband and three young children. Her 31/2 year old daughter Missy came to school one day with a big smile.

During morning sharing time, she raised her hand eagerly, and when I called on her Missy announced with pride, "My daddy goes to bed naked."

Dear Dr. Humor:

My mom told my four year old brother Adam that if anyone should call and ask for her while she is not home, he should simply tell the caller that she could not come to the phone. When a neighbor called for my mom, Adam told the neighbor that my mom could not come to the phone as she was in the shower. When the neighbor asked for my dad, who also was not home, Adam said, "He's in the shower, too."

Dear Dr. Humor:

Twenty years ago, when my brother and sister-in-law were married, they did the traditional thing and preserved the top most layer of their wedding cake to be eaten on their first wedding anniversary.

Like many newlyweds, they lived in a small attic apartment. It was furnished with an old fashioned refrigerator/freezer where the freezer was actually a sub-compartment of the refrigerator that barely held the top layer of their wedding cake. They lived for one year without ice cubes, ice cream, or any frozen food, etc.

On their first anniversary, they carefully defrosted the cake and after a romantic dinner, sliced the cake only to discover that it was made of styrofoam.

Dear Dr. Humor:

I used to be a nursing assistant on the 11 to 7 shift in a nursing home. I did bed checks every two hours and helped residents to the bathroom as needed. During nurses report, I was told a new resident whom I hadn't met yet, toileted herself and used a walker. In the morning I was helping her to get ready for breakfast. She was still in bed and I was going through her closet looking for shoes and stockings. After a frustrating search, I said, "I give up Mrs. Murphy. For some reason I can only find one shoe." Mrs. Murphy responded with a twinkle in her eye, "Honey, I stopped looking for the second shoe fifteen years ago when my foot was amputated."

Dear Dr. Humor:

In the five years my husband and I have been married, he has probably shopped for groceries twice. The first time was shortly after we were married and the second time was recently. Upon filling up the cart and arriving at the check out lane, the cashier asked him if he wanted paper or plastic (referring to the kind of bags). He answered, "Neither, I'll pay by check."

Dear Dr. Humor:

I am a middle school teacher (grades 5 to 8) and I teach a class entitled, "Food and Culture," in which we study and learn about food and peoples all over the world. When I was teaching the U.S. segment, I decided to show selected parts of the movie, "The Alamo" (we had been studying the cultures of Texas and Mexico). When I introduced the film I said, "Does anyone know anything about the Alamo?" Immediately one of my 8th grade students' hand shot up.

"Tell us what you know, Dustin," I said. Dustin answered, "I don't know anything about it, but I know we're supposed to remember it!"

Dear Dr. Humor:

I am principal of a middle school and at the beginning of an inservice to my staff several years ago I wanted to address the issue of our student dress code. A major concern of mine was the attire that our 7th and 8th grade girls were wearing in warm weather. Our general rule said that if the attire caused a disturbance it would be inappropriate. What I said to a staff was:

"I want to spend a minute reviewing our student dress code. As you all know, it will be warm shortly and every year some of the girls don't wear bras. Recently, I have become increasingly aware that this a very sensitive area (meaning a difficult subject to address)." As soon as I got this out, there were a few laughs and snickers. I realized then what I had said and I tried to correct it by saying, "Let me rephrase that. This is a very touchy area." Now the whole group broke up laughing and I truly was embarrassed.

Trying to get the group back on task I finally

said, "I'll get back to you later on this area as to how I want you to handle it." That did it, I lost the group completely and I decided to take a 15 minute break to regain our composure.

Dear Dr. Humor:

Three years ago my husband and I, with two other couples, went on a 7 day Caribbean cruise. We had a wonderful time, the service, the ports and the itinerary were all great. The ship had a movie theater and my husband and I decided to go to an afternoon movie. I laughed so hard when we arrived at the theater and there was a sign put up by a Caribbean member of the crew that said simply, "Next Movie: Tooth-Hirty."

Dear Dr. Humor:

My grandson was staying with me one night. He was having trouble going to sleep so, being the good grandma, I said, "What's the matter?" and he said, "I want someone to come sit by me, I'm lonesome." I said to him, "Don't be lonely, God is always with you." To that my grandson responded, "I know grandma. But I wanted somebody with skin on."

Dear Dr. Humor:

When my oldest child, Lindsay, was 10 years old she became very upset with me and my wife. I don't recall exactly what the incident was but we wouldn't allow her to do something she wanted to do. She said that she was going to run away from home. She ran to her room and several minutes later came out with a grocery bag full of clothes and demanded, "Now, take me to the airport."

It was somewhat prophetic as she is now a flight attendant.

Dear Dr. Humor:

We were traveling from Kansas City to Los Angeles by car for a family vacation several summers ago. We spent one of our over nights in Grand Junction, Colorado. We went out for dinner at a local restaurant. While we were eating we were approached by a man who was soliciting money. We were very suspicious by his appearance and approach that it probably was some kind of scam. What made us particularly suspicious was he said he was collecting for research into a cure for "muscular dysentery."

Dear Dr. Humor:

During the desert storm war there was so much about the war on television. I am a preschool teacher and one morning after snack time we had our large group - we sing, do finger plays, show and tell, etc.

I asked the children, "Who knows what a scud is?" It was quiet for a while and I restated my question, "Does anybody know what a scud is?

One little boy (3 years old) raised his hand and said, "Teacher, I know what a scud is . They're black and white, they run on the road and when you hit them with a car they sure stink."

Dear Dr. Humor:

I saved this article from the police report column of the Bozeman (Montana) Daily Chronicle:

"Domestic problem reported at 5:38 P.M. Tuesday. Woman complained that her 16 year old son was unruly and abusive. The boy was reported to have turned off the television, sat in front of it, and demanded help with his homework. The mother stated to police that she wanted to finish watching 'Scarecrow and Mrs. King' and to be allowed to finish her beer."

Dear Dr. Humor:

A young college student, quite intoxicated, was asked to ride in the back of his friends pick up truck. As they drove down the road he started grabbing safety cones off the road as they passed through a construction zone. He was arrested later and when in court the judge asked, "What would cause you to do such a thing?"

The college student responded in all seriousness to the judge, "Jim Beam, Your Honor."

Dear Dr. Humor:

After receiving an invitation to a wedding, I was explaining to my 5-year-old niece, Angela, how women usually take their husband's last name when they get married. Angela asked what my sister Michele's last name was. My sister Michele had been married three months earlier and Angela and I had both been at the wedding. I did not, however, remember Michele's husband's last name.

Angela said, "I think it is Limousine." "I don't think so," I said. Angela insisted that she was right and when I asked her, "What makes you think it's limousine?" She responded, "Because at the wedding reception, the priest announced to everybody that the limousines are coming."

Dear Dr. Humor:

An elderly woman, who truly loved to shop, recently expired at a woman's shop in a local mall. The local paper carried the story with interviews from the family about her passing away. The family decided to bury her in her favorite sweat shirt, "Shop til you drop." (Journal Times, Racine, WI)

Dear Dr. Humor:

I was in the bathroom, looking in the mirror and feeling sorry for myself. I said to the mirror, "I'm fat and ugly." My little 5 year old sister was with me and very happy to have her older sister home from college (we are very close). In order to make me feel better she said, "You're not ugly, just fat."

Dear Dr. Humor:

When my deaf brother got his first hearing aid at the age of five, we were all confused as to why he kept turning it on and off during the church service. After the service we asked my brother if he was uncomfortable with the hearing aid. He explained that he really liked the hearing aid and that he turned it on during the music but then turned it off during the long advertisements.

Dear Dr. Humor:

Although I am not Catholic, my husband is and when we married I promised to raise our children Catholic. We enrolled our daughter Emily in a Catholic School for first grade. As we learned more about the school it became abundantly clear that the Principal, Sister Agnes, was very much in charge of the school. Although she was small in stature and weighed probably only 90 pounds, she was a strict disciplinarian. She never seemed to raise her voice, but the children were very much aware of the fact that you should never cross Sister Agnes.

At the end of the first week Emily told me that Sister Agnes knew what every child was doing at all times. She also mentioned that Sister Agnes can do miracles. When I asked her what kind of miracles Sister Agnes could do, Emily told me that Sister Agnes can "make her voice come out of the clock."

Dear Dr. Humor:

A woman was preparing food for a very important dinner party. She made a pate out of mushrooms from a recipe she had obtained from the chef of a famous French restaurant. Right before the guests were to arrive, the family dog, who was quite elderly, ate half of the pate´ before she was able to spread it on the crackers. She was faced with the dilemma of whether to serve the remainder and decided to do so and not to tell the guests.

Later in the evening she looked out her front steps to see her dog lying strangely. She went out to check him and determined that he was dead. She concluded that the pate´ must have poisoned the dog and confessed that information to the guests. One of the twelve guests was a physician who called the hospital and immediately arranged for all the guests to have their stomachs pumped. The hosts made arrangements to pay for all the medical treatment.

The next morning the hosts found the

following note in their mailbox, "Dear Neighbor, I am writing to tell you how sorry I am that I ran over your dog. It was an accident. I felt so badly I could not tell you directly but instead decided to put him on the front steps." I heard this story years ago on the Jack Paar Show and have told it many times since.

Dear Dr. Humor:

My daughter's kindergarten teacher shared this story with me about my daughter, Lisa. Lisa is a very conscientious and quiet child.

One day at nap time, her mat was next to her friend Daniel and they were talking instead of resting. Their teacher had to ask them to be quiet.

The next day Lisa was waiting at the door when Daniel arrived. Lisa put her hands on her hips and said, "Daniel, I'm never sleeping with you again, you got me in trouble."

Dear Dr. Humor:

My daughter, who is a student at the University of Minnesota, sent me a copy of a flyer announcing an upcoming meeting that she obtained from the bulletin board in one of the classroom buildings. She and I had a great laugh over it.

The announcement was an invitation by the Minnesota Nutrition Council inviting the public to attend an "all you can eat" luncheon conference. A registered nurse was to be the luncheon speaker and her topic was "Compulsive Overeating."

I'm sure that the "all you can eat" menu was a big draw.

Dear Dr. Humor:

Last year when my daughter completed fourth grade, I asked her if she had thought about what she wanted to be when she grew up. She told me that one of her teachers asked the same thing several days before. They were on a bus while returning from a field trip to the county court house. I asked her what she said to her teacher. She responded, "I told her I was very interested in being a prostituting attorney." She told me that her teacher simply responded with a smile, "That's an interesting combination."

Dear Dr. Humor:

I am the activity director in a large metropolitan nursing home. Humor is a very important part of my job as I laugh with (but not at) the residents. One day I was leading a current events discussion with a group of six ladies. I started out the discussion by saying, "Today we are celebrating the birthday of a famous composer who was born 300 years ago on this date." One of the members of my group gasped and said, "Oh, my, is he bed-ridden?"

Dear Dr. Humor:

I have a very close friend who, throughout the years, has provided me so many real and natural "malaprops" (which I never correct) such as:

One day she was complaining about a pair of slacks she bought which were too tight in the "crouch." In discussing her children, who were sick, she told me that she "dowsed" them with medication. The day after Thanksgiving, she told me that she "gouged" herself at the feast.

Dear Dr. Humor:

I have clipped funny newspaper stories for years. My favorite story occurred in 1971 in Manassas, Virginia. The police apprehended a gentleman who had robbed the local bank. The name of the bank robber was Ernest Moneymaker.

Dear Dr. Humor:

When I was three years old, my grandmother gave me a painting - an original oil painting that was signed by the artist and beautifully framed. It was a Southern Italian scene and I assumed it was a valuable treasure.

My grandmother lived with my aunt and uncle, who were very wealthy and whose house was filled with artistic masterpieces. I had always assumed that they advised my grandmother in her purchases and that grandmother gave me the painting on the assumption that it would be very valuable someday.

The painting went with me to college, in my first apartment, and a location of pride in my first house. Over the years the painting became less meaningful to me and the paint and frame were beginning to fade.

Finally, last year after cherishing the painting for 34 years, I decided to sell it. I took it to my aunt to seek her advise. I carefully took the painting out of the box and removed the bubble wrap I had used to protect it. When I asked my aunt, "What would you suggest I do with this?" She responded, "Give it to the Salvation Army. I never could understand what your Grandmother saw in that awful thing."

Because my aunt is a very formal and proper lady, I did not respond until later when I was driving home with my husband. My husband and I laughed so hard that tears were streaming down our faces.

Dear Dr. Humor:

People say that animals do not have a sense of humor. However, I believe that my observations disprove that conclusion. I have a chihuahua and my father has a german shepherd. We live next door to each other and share a common fence. When I first got my dog, we were fearful that the two dogs would not get along well. They actually became great friends except during feeding, when the german shepherd would try to eat both meals.

We decided each day to separate the dogs for feeding by closing the gate between our yards. That worked fine until one day I forgot to close the gate and the german shepherd came over and took away my dog's steak bone. My little chihuahua barked for a while and then did something quite ingenious. He ran over to a tree and started going around in circles and barking frantically as if he had a squirrel treed. At first the german shepherd ignored him but as the chihuahua persisted, he finally dropped the bone and began to circle the tree and bark also.

Suddenly, my chihuahua abandoned the tree and ran over to where the steak bone was and urinated on the bone.

Dear Dr. Humor:

I am a high school math teacher and I live in a small town in Kansas. There is a very successful lawyer who also lives in the town and has the same first and last name. I believe that a person who called me several weeks ago must have had us confused. Here's what happened:

I was watching television when the phone rang. I answered the phone and had the following conversation:

Caller: "Is this Mr. Nelson, Mr. Carl Nelson?"

Me: "Yes."

Caller: "Please hold for Mr. Watson. (pause) Hello Mr. Nelson, this is Mr. Watson for Fidelity Investments. Have you heard of us?"

Me: "Yes."

Caller: "I'm calling to tell you about a new investment opportunity we've put together especially for people in your line of work. My name's Jack, may I call you Carl?"

Me: "Sure, Jack."

Caller: "Carl, are you in the market now?"

Me: "No."

Caller: "May I ask why?"

Me: "I really haven't been able to afford it."

Caller: "Do you plan to invest $1,000 to $5,000 over the next year?"

Me: "I'd like to but I don't think so."

Caller: "Carl, may I ask why?"

Me: "You see, Jack, I'm a high school teacher and . . . "

Caller: "Excuse me, I don't mean to interrupt, but you said you were a teacher?"

Me: "Yes."

Caller: "Well, good luck to you, sir." (Click)

Dear Dr. Humor:

I was flying from Charlotte, North Carolina, to Chicago last September. I fly on business a great deal and normally I don't expect weather problems in September. Unfortunately, Chicago was fogged in and we had been in a holding pattern for about 45 minutes. The pilot announced over the intercom system. "Ladies and gentlemen, I am pleased to announce that we have just been cleared to land." The passengers all clapped in good spirits. The pilot then added, "Three out of the last seven have made it."

The cabin became immediately stone quiet and then several people began to inquire about exactly what he had said (I believe they were hoping that they misunderstood him). The lady I was sitting next to started quietly to pray.

The pilot then said, "Ladies and gentlemen, I apologize for any confusion I may have caused with my previous announcement. I neglected to inform you that the four planes that didn't make it were rerouted to Milwaukee."

Dear Dr. Humor:

I am the financial aids officer for a private college. The tuition for students to attend is quite high and over 65% of our student body is on some kind of financial aid. I have on my office wall a framed financial aid application form that I received several years ago from a freshman female student. She had completed the long application form and in the part of the form that asked her to answer the following question, "What's the approximate net worth of your parents?" she wrote, "Priceless."

Dear Dr. Humor:

My wife is an artist and shared this wonderful story about the famous painter, Maxfield Parrish who died in 1966. Parrish was the illustrator of the Arabian Nights. Apparently Mr. Parrish was a very prolific painter, although he complained as he was getting older that he had a difficult time getting started but that once he did start each day he would spend hours painting.

One morning a beautiful professional model arrived at his studio to pose for him. Parrish decided that he didn't feel like working and suggested that they sit together and have a cup of coffee. As they were sitting and visiting, the doorbell to his studio rang and he heard his wife's voice announcing that she was coming upstairs.

Mr. Parrish then apparently yelled to the model, "Hurry and take your clothes off, my wife is coming to check on me."

Dear Dr. Humor:

I attended a Rotary meeting one week in which we had the coach of a local and very successful college football team. He began his speech by saying, "My grandfather always told me that an after dinner speech should never be longer than it takes a man to make love. I didn't really understand that when I was a small boy, but I think I do now....so in conclusion." He received very loud applause.

Dear Dr. Humor:

Not long after my husband Jack was made senior vice-president of marketing for a fortune 500 company, we invited the president of the company, Bill Sullivan and his wife Mary over for dinner.

Before they arrived, I spoke to my children ages 5 and 8 about being well behaved and using good manners. I was particularly concerned about my oldest son, Jason, saying something or staring at Mr. Sullivan's exceedingly large bulbous red nose.

I fed the children before the Sullivans arrived and rented several videos to keep them occupied while we had dinner. The children were ushered in to meet the Sullivans after we had eaten and were about to have our dessert. I was very relieved as the children were angels and very well behaved. As I got up to excuse myself to put them to bed I said to the company president, "Bill, would you care for cream or sugar for your nose?"

Dear Dr. Humor:

When my daughter Betsy was 4 years old, I picked her up from pre-school and we went home for lunch. After Betsy completed her lunch and I gave her six M&M's for dessert, we had the following conversation:

"Mommy, we learned about candy in school today. We had a policeman who told about good strangers and bad strangers and not to take candy from bad strangers." She went on to tell me the difference between good and bad strangers and answered several other questions I had asked her.

Finally, I asked her, "Betsy, if a bad stranger offered you candy, what would you say?" She responded, "I'd say I'm sorry but I can't accept candy from a bad stranger, you got any fruit?"

Dear Dr. Humor:

During college, I worked on tugboats on the Mississippi River for a summer job. I would be assigned as a floater to work on different trips where additional holp was needed, generally rotating tugs every several weeks.

On one trip the captain was very strict and a stickler for detail. Following a night where the tug was tied up along the bank for the evening and the crew did a little late night partying, the captain entered into the log the next morning, "The first mate was drunk last night."

Seeing this the first mate was very upset and begged the captain to remove the comment from the log. He reminded the captain that he does not drink often and had been off duty during the evening. The first mate was very concerned about the impact that statement would have on his career.

The captain indicated that it was a fact that the first mate was drunk, the record would stand as it is the obligation of the captain and those who desire to be captain someday to always be absolutely factual in reporting.

Several nights later as the tug pushed its barges north toward Minneapolis, the first mate was assigned the evening watch. The next morning the captain was furious as the first mate had entered into the log, "The captain was sober last night."

Dear Dr. Humor:

Three years ago my husband, my three sons and I were on our way to a Minnesota Vikings football game. Our entire family are Viking nuts and we haven't missed a home game in years. This particular Sunday it was -22 degrees with a wind chill of 47 below, and we were running late. I drove and offered to drop my husband and three boys off close to the stadium so they could be there for the kickoff as I parked the car.

Later during the first half, my husband, who is a surgeon, was paged on the public address system to call the hospital. He called and decided that he needed to go right away to the hospital to check on a patient. I gave him the car keys and he asked me where I parked the car. I could only remember it was in the stadium parking lot but not what section.

We contacted stadium security officers and told them of our problems. They were wonderful and had seven security officers looking up and down the rows for our car. I had described the

133

car as a 1989 white Plymouth Voyager and had provided the license plate number. After some 45 minutes they were able to locate the car and the head of security drove us to the car. We thanked him many times over, offered him a tip (which he refused) and as he dropped us off he said:

"Lady, next time you lose your car in -22 weather and you are asked to describe it, it's helpful to tell us the make, color, year, and license plate number. But it might have been even more helpful if you had told us about the lime green canoe on top."

Dear Dr. Humor:

I was employed in middle management at Star-Kist Foods in Long Beach, California in 1983. All 35 of us were sent to an intense management training seminar in Kansas City for a week. The seminar focused on management functions including planning, organizing, leading, controlling, and delegating. It was an exhausting, but productive, week and we were all flying back together on a Friday evening.

We experienced a great deal of turbulence on the way home. The captain, in a calm voice, advised passengers to fasten their seatbelts and told the attendants to take their seats.

We were in a very rough storm and we could see lightning all around us. All of us were truly frightened. My buddy saw a priest sitting several rows in front of us and yelled to him, "Father, can't you do something about this?"

The priest calmly replied, "Sorry, that's operations. I'm in marketing."

Dear Dr. Humor:

Fourteen years ago my father passed away at the age of 74. He was a retired army officer and was buried at Arlington National Cemetery in Washington. Mom wasn't doing very well and had not eaten or slept very well for several days prior to the service. My five-year-old son, Bradley, was all dressed up in a dark blue military looking suit for the funeral which he picked out in honor of his granddad.

After the service at the chapel, we drove to the grave site. We neglected to tell Bradley that there would be 21 gun salute in honor of dad at the grave site. We had a small service at the grave site, and dear old mom was barely hanging on when she fainted at the same time as the first round of the guns went off. Bradley turned and yelled very loud to all, "Call the FBI, someone shot grandma."

Dear Dr. Humor:

My 9-year-old nephew and I went shopping in search of a Chicago Cubs baseball hat. He was to use his allowance to make the purchase. We went into a department store and he directed me to the boys department where he found the hat he wanted and we proceeded to check out.

He hesitated for a long time at the checkout counter. It was quite obvious he was hoping that I'd pay for the hat. When I didn't, he reluctantly pulled out a ten dollar bill that he gave the cashier. She gave him 19 cents change and we began to leave he store.

I said to him, in an effort to use this opportunity to teach him the value of money, "See, Kyle, it doesn't take long to spend ten dollars, does it?" He responded, "No, not when you know exactly what you're looking for."

Dear Dr. Humor:

In the late 1950's, my father owned a hardware store in Perry, Iowa, a town of approximately 7,000. He didn't make much money. Thus, our family was rarely able to go to the big city of Des Moines to go out to a fine restaurant.

After saving up some money and being bored, Dad decided to take our family of six (two boys, two girls, Mom and Dad) to the big city for a nice dinner at a popular restaurant. My oldest brother, Tommy (age 6 at the time), had to go to the bathroom to relieve himself. So, being a good father, Dad took him to the bathroom.

Tommy apparently was finished with his "business" first and, as he opened the bathroom door, he yelled across the restaurant, "Hey Mom, Dad just peed in the sink." Tommy had never seen a urinal before in his life.

Dear Dr. Humor:

My grandfather told me a wonderful story I thought you would enjoy. He was from Topeka, Kansas and in 1948 the state of Kansas had condemned downtown property to build a new highway. In that particular part of town there were three men's clothing stores next to each other. One Monday morning, the owner of the middle store came to work and noticed that the store on one side had the following sign, "Bankruptcy Sale - All Merchandise Must Go," and the store on the other side had a sign in the window that read, "Closing Out Sale - Everything At Cost." Twenty minutes later the owner of the middle store put up the following sign "Main Entrance."

Dear Dr. Humor:

I work for the Red Cross and was teaching first aide to a group of preschoolers. The first three lessons included how to care for wounds, bee stings and burns. The kids were very attentive and responded well to the questions I asked after each lesson.

The fourth lesson was on what to do if you swallow something that might be harmful. One of the children volunteered that her baby brother had swallow a quarter. I asked the class, "What do you think you should do if you swallow a coin?" One of the children answered in all seriousness, "You should call our priest because my Dad told me that he could get money out of anyone."

Dear Dr. Humor:

I live in Tarrytown, New York, on the Hudson River and commute daily into New York City. I typically walk to and from the train station, a distance of approximately one mile. Last summer I had a very unnerving experience that turned out to be funny.

I got off the train around 7:45 pm and as I was walking home I heard footsteps behind me. I had a very uncomfortable feeling that I was being followed so I increased my speed. The footsteps behind me also increased in speed. As I became more frightened, I started running and jumped over a fence, landed in a neighbor's yard and hid behind a large patch of bushes.

The person was right behind me and I heard him scrambling over the fence also. I really was in fear for my life when a voice called out to me, "Where are you Mr. Williams?" the voice went on, "Please don't be afraid of me."

My knees were literally shaking when I said, "What do you want and why are you following me?" The man responded that he had asked for directions from one of the commuters to the Coburn's house and the commuter had told him to follow me as I lived next door. We both had a good laugh about that incident.

Dear Dr. Humor:

My father is a Political Science Professor at a large state university. For years he has made a point of reading the Congressional Record looking for amusing anecdotes of which he has quite a collection. He uses them to spice up his lectures.

One of his favorite stories involved Congressman Johnson of Indiana who, in the Congressional Record, referred to his counterpart from Illinois in the heat of an intense debate, as a "jackass." Later, Congressman Johnson, while issuing a retraction, said, "While I withdraw the unfortunate choice of words, Mr. Speaker, I must insist the gentleman from Illinois is out of order."

The Congressman from Illinois responded, "Out of order? How am I out of order?" To which Johnson responded on the record, "That information, sir, would have to be supplied by a veterinary surgeon."

Dear Dr. Humor:

The following letter was adapted from a 1946 book entitled "Dear Sir or Madam" by Juliet Lowell. It was a sequel to her first book "Dear Sir" published in 1943 which sold over 400,000 copies and was designed to provide war weary readers with rich humor at a time when humor was priceless.

April 7, 1941
Mr. Harold Johnson
New York Taxidermy Services
New York, New York

Dear Mr. Johnson,

In reply to your letter about my two hunting dogs which I accidentally shot and sent to you to be stuffed. You asked if I want them mounted. No, please don't mount them. Just have them side by side as they were only friends.

Sincerely yours,

Dear Dr. Humor:

Approximately 15 years ago we had a cat, Samantha, who had very distinctive color markings. One day I received a call from my wife who was crying and informed me that Samantha had been run over and was lying on a major highway several blocks from home.

I left work and drove to the spot and sure enough, Samantha was lying there "flat as a pancake." I went home, picked up a box and shovel and told my wife to make sure that our young son was not near any window as I intended to bury Samantha in our backyard.

When I picked up Samantha it was impossible to get all her remains in the box as rigor mortis had set in and her legs were stiff and they stuck straight up in the air. I carried the box to the far reaches of our property, dug a deep hole, buried Samantha, and placed a large boulder as a marker. I remember thinking at the time about how or what we would tell our son who was very attached to Samantha.

As I picked up the box and shovel and started walking toward the house, there on the wall that separated our yard from our neighbors', walking rather nonchalantly, was Samantha. I realized that I just buried someone else's DEAD CAT !!

Dear Dr. Humor:

I have a three-year-old daughter named Amy. We were standing in line at an elementary school, waiting to vote on a referendum for our school district and she asked if she could go play on the mats with the other children.

I told her that she could not play with the other children as I didn't know those other kids, and I wanted her to stay in line with me.

So, being the good 3-year-old she is, she promptly faced forward and stood in line. I was watching her and I realized that she was butt level ... or face level, or however you want to put it - to the man in front of her.

She was looking directly at his butt - and suddenly she started leaning forward, and she was about an inch away from this man's butt. And she starts sniffing!

I'm standing there in horror, thinking, "What is my daughter doing?" She's sniffing, and she's sniffing, and she turns her little head around and says, "Hey, Mom!"

I said, "What?" She responded, "Come here." So I bend over, and I'm now face-level with this man's butt, and she says, "Smell this guy's butt!" I was mortified and couldn't wait to get out of there.

Dear Dr. Humor:

When our two girls were young, about ages three and five, I was involved in making some dolls for a church bazaar. I was way behind schedule in making the dolls and enlisted the help of my husband to stuff them with foam.

We told the girls to stay upstairs while we worked in the basement. The phone rang, my youngest daughter took the call and said that it was "nothing." A few minutes later the door bell rang. I came upstairs and answered the door, it was our pastor - laughing hysterically. He was the one who called and when he asked to speak to my husband or myself, my three-year-old told him that we were both in the basement making babies.

Dear Dr. Humor:

My six-year-old daughter, Cindy, and I had the following conversation one morning at breakfast.

Cindy: "Mom, my friends at school told me that you are the tooth fairy. Is that true?"

Me: "You know, I always tell you the truth. Are you sure you're ready for the answer to that question?"

Cindy: "Yes, Mommy, I really want to know."

Me: "It's true honey, I am the tooth fairy."

Cindy: "Well, then Mom, what do you do with all the other children's teeth?"

Dear Dr. Humor:

I am an Iowa Deputy Sheriff and was on my way to visit my parents in Wisconsin. I was driving on the interstate when a State Trooper pulled behind me. The speed limit was 65 and I was doing 73. I slowed down to 60 hoping that he would pass me but instead he also slowed down to 60 and followed me for about 10 miles. I kept looking in the rear view mirror and was getting pretty nervous.

Finally I decided to increase my speed to 65 mph and as I was accelerating, a pheasant flew out in front of me, hit the hood of my van, flipped over the top and splattered all over the trooper's windshield. The trooper immediately turned on his red lights and siren and motioned for me to pull over. I obeyed his command. He walked up to my van and asked to see my driver's license. I politely asked him what I had done wrong and he said he was going to give me warning for "flipping me the bird."

Dear Dr. Humor:

I had a routine checkup with my gynecologist one morning at 11:30. I received a call from his office that morning around 8:45 telling me that there had been a cancellation and asking if I could come in at 9:30, which I agreed to do.

The trip to the doctor's office takes about 35 minutes so I didn't have much time. As most women do, I like to take a little extra effort over hygiene on these kind of visits. So I rushed upstairs, threw off my pajamas, wet a washcloth and gave myself a wash in "that area", put on my clothes and raced off to my appointment.

When I arrived I was immediately ushered into the examining room. Being familiar with the procedure, I got up on the table, closed my eyes, and pretended I was in Hawaii. I was a little confused when he doctor said: "My . . . we've taken a little extra effort this morning, haven't we?" I didn't know what he was talking about so I didn't respond.

The rest of the day was pretty normal until about 6:30 that evening and my 14 years old-daughter was getting ready to go to a school dance. She called down from the bathroom, "Mom, where is my washcloth?" I told her that I had used it and to get herself another one. She called back, No, Mom – I need the one that was here by the sink, it had all my gold glitter and sparkles in it.

Dear Dr. Humor:

I live in Sydney, Australia and I would love to join your organization. This story happened to my next door neighbors last Tuesday. Joe and Mary Simpson drove their car to K-Mart only to have the car break down in the parking lot. Joe told his wife to go ahead and shop and he would try to repair the car.

When Mary returned after 45 minutes she found a small group of people had gathered around the car. On closer inspection, she saw a pair of male legs protruding from under the chassis. He was wearing shorts and his lack of underpants turned his private parts into public exposure.

To protect her husband from further embarrassment, Mary quickly put her hand up his shorts and tucked everything back into place. When she stood up and looked across the hood of her car, she found herself staring at her husband.

P.S. The mechanic had to have three stitches in his head.

Dear Dr. Humor:

I left Montreal on Route 20 heading toward Quebec City, when I decided to stop at a comfort station. The first toilet stall was occupied so I went into the second one. I was no sooner seated then I heard a voice from the next stall:

"Hi, how are you doing?"

I answered, a little embarrassed, "Not bad."

And the stranger then asked: "And what are you up to?"

Talk about stupid questions! So I said: "Well, just like you I'm driving east."

Then I heard the stranger, all upset, say: "Look I'll call you back later — there's some jerk in the next stall answering all my questions!"

Dear Dr. Humor:

The principal of our middle school in Beaverton, Oregon had a problem with a few of the older girls when they started using lipstick. The girls would apply their lipstick in the bathroom and then press their lips to the mirror, some days leaving over 40 lips prints on the mirror. Before it got too far out of hand, the Principal thought of a very clever solution.

One day, he gathered all the girls together that wore lipstick and told them he wanted to meet them in the girls' bathroom. They all gathered at the appointed time and found the principal and custodian waiting for them.

The principal explained that it was becoming a major problem for the custodian to clean the mirror each night and still get the rest of his work done. He said he felt the ladies would be more supportive if they understood what was involved. He then asked the custodian to demonstrate.

The custodian then took out a large brush, dipped it in the toilet, and proceeded to wipe the mirror – that was the last day the girl pressed their lips to the mirror.

Dear Dr. Humor:

When I was 8 years old my family moved from New York to North Carolina. I'm very Irish and I really stood out among my new classmates. The first week of school I came home in tears because the kids were making fun of my red hair and my pasty white skin. I told my grandfather that another boy had called me a racial slur.

My grandfather, whom I adored, said: "Sean, don't be blaming it on your skin color or your racial background. You're going to meet lots of people in this world who won't like you, simply because you're irritating."

REFERENCES

Norman Cousins (1989) <u>Head First: The Biology of Hope</u>. E.P. Dutton: New York.

Christian Hageseth(1988) <u>A Laughing Place</u>. Berwick Publ. Co: Fort Collins, CO.

Eric Johnson (1991) <u>Humorous Stories About The Human Condition</u>. Prometheus Books: Buffalo, N.Y.

Allen Klein (1989) <u>The Healing Power of Humor</u>. Jeremy Tarcher, Inc.: Los Angeles, CA.

C. W. Metcalf and Roma Felible (1992) <u>Lighten Up: Survival Skills for People Under Pressure</u>. Addison-Wesley: Reading, MA.